THE SCIENCE OF ANSWERED PRAYERS

WRITTEN BY

HEPHZIBAH FRANCES

Unless otherwise indicated, all scripture quotations are taken from the New King James Version of the Bible. All rights reserved. Used by permission.

THE SCIENCE OF ANSWERED PRAYERS.

Copyright ©2021 by Hephzibah Frances

okorofrances@gmail.com

www.hephzibahfrances.com

Book cover design & Publishing done by:

BEAUTIFUL FEET PUBLISHING

beautifulfeetpublishing@gmail.com

+2347035539092

CONTENT

DEDICATION

"O You who hear prayer, To You all flesh will come."

-Psalm 65:2

ACKNOWLEDGEMENTS

To the Holy Spirit; the One who helps me in my weaknesses. Thank You! I Love You! Thank You!

INTRODUCTION

*"But our God is in heaven; He does
whatever He pleases.*

-Psalm 115:3

I have always been fascinated with the subject of prayer. My fascination with this subject never gets old and every time I pray and see results, I find myself amazed with this amazing tool of heaven touching earth called *prayer.*

My first encounter with the amazing tool of prayer happened the night I got born again.

I got born again one night in July 2011 in the midst of having a terrible quarrel with my then boyfriend. We were in the midst of a stupid argument when suddenly; I reached my 'boiling or turning point' (as you will soon see). I suddenly got blasted by the stupidity of the quarrel we were having; *was this what girls my age had to go through?* It felt like I was too young to be involved in what I was involved in at the time and there just may be a better life way out there for me. So right there and then, sitting on the floor in front of my then boyfriend, I turned my attention to God and started crying out to

Him. I cried with everything in me; catarrh running down my nose – I didn't care. I said *"Lord, if you want me to be in this relationship, tell me tonight or if you want me to leave, also tell me tonight. Tonight Lord. Tell me now Lord".*

And God answered.

Suddenly it felt like someone had wrapped his hands around me in a hug. I felt loved and I felt accepted all at the same time. And I also felt strength come and take a hold of me. That strength made me stand up and walk away from that scene with my then boyfriend. By the time I woke up in the morning, I woke up with a radical love and hunger for Jesus. A divine surgery had gone on in the night while I slept. I never did return back to that relationship again and my life has continued to blossom in God ever since. Glory to God! Hallelujah!

This was my first experience with how to touch heaven through prayer.

I didn't even know it then but it would become a pattern after then in my life where I would pray and see results. I literally would see that God answered me! Me! God answered me.

I mean tangible results like my brother's salvation through prayer, getting a law school internship I wasn't qualified for through prayer, getting finances through prayer, hearing God's voice through prayer, getting deliverance through prayer, seeing the revival of the Holy Ghost fall through prayer... it became a lot and I am still asking for more! There is nothing else that ignites your faith so much as to see that wow! While I was speaking here on earth, God in heaven heard me and sent the answer back to me on the earth!

Wow! Such a privilege we have been given through this magnificent weapon of prayer and supplication.

> *"So Cornelius said, "Four days ago I*
>
> *was fasting until this hour; and at the*
>
> *ninth hour I prayed in my house, and*
>
> *behold, a man stood before me in bright*
>
> *clothing, and said, "Cornelius, your prayer has*
>
> *been heard, and your alms are*
>
> *remembered in the sight of God."*
>
> *-Acts 10:30-31*

What a joy it is to hear those words: your prayers have been heard!

And as we would see soon, those words do not only come in the form of angelic visitation but there is a recognizing system God has put in us to let us know when our prayers have been heard.

This book may be short but it would be a very powerful tool for reigniting your prayer life to see results.

You will learn a few things God has taught me in the last few years of seeking Him – my God in heaven in prayer – and seeing His answer sent to me on the earth.

It is my prayer that as you read, you come to marvel at the marvelous wonder of the gift called prayer and not just marvel alone, but plunge deeply into it, take all your friends and family members in with you as you see that our God may be in heaven, He does whatever He pleases, but He sure can do whatever He pleases in your favour through the gift of prayer that has been made available unto you.

His wonders are made available to us on the earth through the powerful weapon of prayer.

Hephzibah Frances

TWTW House Of Grace,

Lagos, Nigeria

18th January 2021

CHAPTER ONE
CARRYING AND YIELDING TO THE BURDEN OF PRAYER

*"So I sought for a man among them
who would make a wall, and stand in the
gap before Me on behalf of the land,
that I should not destroy it; but I found
no one.
Therefore I have poured out My
indignation on them; I have consumed
them with the fire of My wrath; and I
have recompensed their deeds on their
own heads," says the Lord GOD."*

-Ezekiel 22:30-31

Definition of burden:

A heavy load weighing on a person.

God Himself carries burdens on His heart – burden for people, families, businesses, organizations, nations etc. He sees the cry of these persons even if they may not see their issues with wide open eyes by themselves and He desires to help them but the only authorized medium through which God can legally step into a man's life is through the altar of prayer.

> *"The heaven, even the heavens, are*
> *the LORD's; But the earth He has given*
> *to the children of men."*
>
> *-Psalm 115:18*

God created the earth and gave the keys to the children of men; in other words He gave the keys to you and I. Satan organized a coup in heaven in Genesis chapter 3 that saw the keys of the earth being passed to Him but God on the other hand sent the Lord Jesus Christ who then took the keys of the earth and passed over to us who are children of God.

> *"And Jesus came and spoke to them,*
> *saying, "All authority has been given to*
> *Me in heaven and on earth.*
> *Go therefore and make disciples of all*
> *the nations, baptizing them in the name*
> *of the Father and of the Son and of the*
> *Holy Spirit,*
> *teaching them to observe all things*
> *that I have commanded you; and lo, I*
> *am with you always, even to the end of*
> *the age." Amen."*
>
> *-Matthew 28:18-20*

Jesus took back the keys of authority both of heaven and of the earth and then passed it over to us.

Stop right there.

If you are a born again child of God, Jesus gave the authority God gave Him on the earth and in heaven to you.

But we only wield this authority through prayer.

Let me tell you what prayer is…

Prayer is the means by which God steps into the earth, taking the form of whatever it is we have called Him to do for us. It is like an elevator through which God passes straight from heaven to the earth to do for us what we have asked for. But we cannot pray without a burden. Meaning that, there must be something burning in our hearts as it burns in God's heart that leads us to pray. If we pray without a burden, we would simply be rattling off prayers by rote that do not move us and so cannot move God.

God is not an unfeeling person.

*"For we do not have a High Priest who
cannot sympathize with our weaknesses,
but was in all points tempted as we are,
yet without sin."*

-Hebrews 4:15

God feels pains. God laughs and Jesus weeps.

Jesus weeps over cities. Jesus weeps over families. Jesus weeps over Nations. He weeps at what He sees happening in, to and with them but He cannot intervene except there is someone on earth who is feeling that burden with Him and He does not just spurt off his mouth about it, but carries that burden in prayer to God, the One who can do all things to work through the power of prayer being offered unto Him.

This is the way of the Kingdom of God.

In 1ˢᵗ Samuel chapter 1, we see Hannah, the woman who had been barren for many years being taunted by her husband's other wife, Peninnah. Hannah simply carried that burden of not having children in her heart without talking to God about it, year after year after year. But the year she finally took that burden in prayer to God, praying according to His will, boom! Things happened! (please read the whole chapter of 1st Samuel 1 to see this).

When you carry a burden for prayer, it means something about a situation is weighing heavily on your heart. I have carried burdens in prayer for myself, my family members, ministry, nations, etc. and I have seen wonderful things happen when I took that burden in prayer and prayed it through. One of the most amazing testimonies was the testimony of how my brother gave his life to Christ (I relate this in my book *The Science Of Interceding For The Salvation of Your Loved Ones*).

A burden is meant to lead you to prayer but you have to yield to that burden. Sometimes God may give a family member a burden, which can even come through a dream. Maybe you had a dream that a loved one died but you just woke up, and didn't pray about that burden. You simply spoke about it; it weighed heavily on your heart but you never prayed about it till you prayed through; then when that loved one dies, you say "and I saw this in my dream". You saw it in your dream because God trusted you to go through the altar of prayer to change the outcome of what the enemy had already planned against your loved one.

The authority Jesus gave to us spreads towards changing things we don't want to see to fit into the original will of God as it is in heaven. If there is something happening in your family you don't like, that is a burden, take that burden in prayer and begin to pray about it.

How do you pray about it?

We will talk about that in the next chapter but for now, what is terribly important for you to get is that, for you to get the fullness of the power of praying prayers that get results, you have to yield to the burdens God has put in your heart. In other words, you have to pray. You have to get a quiet spot dedicated to prayer and supplication. That spot can be anywhere in your house where you know you won't be distracted and take that burden in prayer and pray.

Now let's talk about how to pray.

CHAPTER TWO
THE SPIRIT ALSO HELPS OUR WEAKNESSES

"Likewise the Spirit also helps in our weaknesses. For we do not know what we should pray for as we ought, but the Spirit Himself makes intercession for us with groanings which cannot be uttered. Now He who searches the hearts knows what the mind of the Spirit is, because He makes intercession for the saints according to the will of God. And we know that all things work together for good to those who love God, to those who are the called according to His purpose."

-Romans 8:26-28

Now this is the truth: you cannot intercede for a burden in the right way without the Holy Spirit.

The Holy Spirit is the Spirit of prayer and supplication.

The Holy Spirit is also the custodian of the thoughts of God. The Holy Spirit is the only one who knows what the Father is thinking per time. You don't know what God is thinking except the Holy Spirit reveals it to you.

> *"But as it is written: "Eye has not seen, nor ear heard, Nor have entered into the heart of man The things which God has prepared for those who love Him."*
> *But God has revealed them to us through His Spirit. For the Spirit searches all things, yes, the deep things of God.*
> *For what man knows the things of a man except the spirit of the man which is in him? Even so no one knows the things of God except the Spirit of God. Now we have received, not the spirit of the world, but the Spirit who is from God, that we might know the things that have been freely given to us by God."*
>
> *-1st Corinthians 2:9-12*

The things of God cannot be seen by the natural eye, neither can they be heard by the natural ears. The Holy Spirit is the only person who is authorized to know the things of God. What this means is that the Holy Spirit is the only person who knows God's mind about a matter and you cannot get God's mind about a matter except the Holy Spirit reveals it to you.

So when we come to the issue of praying prayers that get results, the only type of prayers that get answered are prayers that are prayed according to the will of God but you can't know the will of God except the Holy Ghost shows you the will of God.

I once heard a story that is a great illustration of this truth.

In this story, a certain woman was being owed a lot of money by somebody who was refusing to pay. She had prayed and prayed all sorts of prayer. Lord give them no rest till they pay me my money etc. Finally while gathered in prayer with others one day, the person she was praying with said she felt led that God would have them pray and release His peace into that person's life. It was such a strange prayer because what you want isn't peace but that they should get restless enough to pay the money being owed. But they obeyed the Holy Spirit and prayed the prayer they felt led to pray. Sure enough, in no long amount of time, that person ran to them to pay them the money being owed for such a long time.

This is the perfect illustration for getting results in prayer by praying according to the will of God.

When you pray for the will of God concerning an issue, you will always get answers but you need the Holy Spirit to know the will of God.

This is how I approach prayer. I approach prayer in humility, knowing that I don't know what to pray for as I ought.

I have been approaching prayer this way after I became baptized in the Holy Spirit with evidence of speaking in tongues but the full impact of praying this way did not dawn on me until the year 2018 when the Lord led me to start hosting eight hours tongues prayer sessions. I had never stretched in prayer for this long before. I didn't have a prayer list long enough to fill eight hours of prayer, and I was inviting people to come for this prayer meeting where I did not know what we were going to pray for.

So I would begin each meeting in humility before God, asking the Holy Spirit to please come and pray for us according to the mind and will of the Father and He would come. Sometimes it would be a scripture He would give to us to pray; sometimes He would remind us of a circumstance and raise a prayer point etc. but all in all, for each of those prayer times, sometimes we lasted as much ten hours in prayer and we still had no shortage for what to pray for, totally being led by the Holy Spirit to pray what was in the Lord's heart for us and there were no shortage of testimonies both for the women in our ministry and myself included.

At the very first prayer meeting where prior to that meeting God had been speaking to me about traveling to Ghana; I had no connections nor money for the trip but by the time we ended prayer, I had more than enough and connections also from everywhere. It happened with such speed in one day of praying according to the will of God.

I can go on and on sharing testimonies of this kind in

my life.

What I would suggest, if you really want to pray prayers that get answered and get results from God, is to go in humility before God, asking for the help and power of the Holy Spirit in prayer.

Start as I start by mentioning the issue before God; Lord we have so and so happening and we truly need your intervention…"

And then ask the Holy Spirit to come help you pray according to the will of God. Tell Him "Precious Holy Spirit, I don't know how to pray about this matter, please help me pray according to the will of God concerning this issue…"

And then start to speak in tongues, your God-given language given to you by God.

*"For he who speaks in a tongue does
not speak to men but to God, for no one
understands him; however, in the spirit
he speaks mysteries."*

-1st Corinthians 14:3

When you speak in tongues, you are speaking directly to God in a language that only Him understands and you are also speaking mysteries concerning that matter; what hasn't been told to you but is in God's heart about the issue.

After a while you might actually begin to have an understanding of what you are saying. E.g., a scripture verse may come to mind

God would ask you to declare concerning that issue or phrases may bubble up that you start to say out loud as you pray… God is revealing to you His very own solution in prayer concerning that issue and since it's exactly what is in the Lord's heart, you are sure to get results.

Now, more often than not when you pray like this, the Holy Spirit would give you a word from scripture you can use in prayer. Why this is so is because God works everything He works by the power of His word. The word of God and the Spirit of God therefore works hand in hand, together, to bring to pass God's answers concerning your prayer.

> *"For there are three that bear witness in heaven: the Father, the Word, and the Holy Spirit; and these three are one."*
>
> *-1ˢᵗ John 5:7*

Everything is inter-tied in its operations.

God the Father is at the very head of that operation who gives the word/decree for what is to be done concerning that prayer. The word is Jesus essentially who is sent into that situation. That word is caused to come to pass by the power of the Spirit. Somewhere in the midst of this is also the ministry of angels who go with power to do God's bidding and we know that power also comes from the Holy Spirit – dunamis power that shifts things and makes things happen.

The trinity – God the Father, Son and the Holy Ghost – are all connected in bringing answers to you in this beautiful tapestry called prayer. But first you must start with the Holy Ghost. Don't go into prayer, just blabbing away with what you think you need and is the answer to that situation. Yes, God is our Father and sometimes we just go to Him to talk to Him and make our desires known and He answers that too because He is our Father but that is a different dimension of prayer.

Here, we are talking about the road and pathway God has created for answers to prayer through simply knowing His will and praying that will to come to pass concerning any situation at all that's standing before you. If you truly want results in prayer, this is the way to go.

Now let's talk about the very next thing in this same dimension of prayer in praying burdens till they become tangible answers to prayers that we can see on the earth.

CHAPTER THREE
PRAYING BURDENS THROUGH

*"And I will pour on the house of David
and on the inhabitants of Jerusalem the
Spirit of grace and supplication; then
they will look on Me whom they pierced.
Yes, they will mourn for Him as one
mourns for his only son, and grieve for
Him as one grieves for a firstborn.
In that day there shall be a great
mourning in Jerusalem, like the
mourning at Hadad Rimmon in the plain
of Megiddo.
And the land shall mourn, every family
by itself: the family of the house of David
by itself, and their wives by themselves;
the family of the house of Nathan by
itself, and their wives by themselves;
the family of the house of Levi by itself,
and their wives by themselves; the
family of Shimei by itself, and their wives
by themselves;
all the families that remain, every
family by itself, and their wives by
themselves."*

-Zechariah 12:10-14

Do you understand what the Lord is saying? The scripture above is the most descriptive form of the Spirit of intercession I have ever seen.

You need the Spirit of intercession to pray burdens through in prayer. Without this empowerment by the Spirit, all you have may just be mere words.

As I write the words I hear is "Holy Spirit take a hold together with me and pray this through".

Now, when burdens come upon a man, they come sometimes like a cloak of heaviness. A deep pain in one's heart concerning a particular situation and sometimes even without praying about it, you find yourself shedding tears because you are so pained about it.

> *"And when he drew near and saw*
> *the city, he wept over it,..."*
>
> *-Luke 19:41*

Now this was Jesus weeping from the pain of the burden in His heart concerning Jerusalem. What the Holy Spirit does is that, when you carry this kind of burden to prayer and ask the Holy Spirit to pray about it according to the will of God, you may find yourself weeping in prayer, doubling over in pain, sometimes you leave the realm of praying coherent words into groanings.

> **"For we do not know what**
> **we should pray for as we ought, but the**
> **Spirit Himself makes intercession for us**
> **with groanings which cannot be uttered."**

-Romans 8:27

The Holy Spirit is the one doing this, praying through this burden through you. Sometimes it is so intense, maybe it's the salvation of someone you are interceding for, you almost feel lost yourself. The Holy Spirit has brought you into true intercession about that matter and as you weep and cry in prayer, if God can open your eyes to see, you are literally in the court of heaven processing that matter through, before God. God has allowed you through the help of the Holy Spirit, to take your place before Him to plead that case.

The most important thing in this realm of praying prayer burdens through the help of the Spirit of intercession is to not stop midway.

God is known as the judge of all the earth. His court system is very much like our earthly system where people come to plead their case. Satan comes too to accuse the brethren. Jesus is seated in the courtroom also as the one who lives to make intercession for us and the Holy Spirit is also our advocate. When we intercede in this way, where a heavy burden of intercession is upon us and we find ourselves groaning before the courts of heaven, our case is being pleaded before God and all sorts of things may be going on about that matter. Satan may be bringing accusations against us, angels that had been dispensed may be held back by demonic forces, accusations from our past may be springing up concerning us, and the Holy Spirit may be processing answers from the mouth of God to get to us. Whatever may be going on as we intercede in prayer this way, you don't want to stop it midway; it has to be processed through to the end.

How do you know you are at the end and have prayed through that situation?

All of a sudden the tears may turn to laughter, or you actually may find yourself laughing and crying at the same time. Or a sudden burst of thanksgiving erupts out of you. Or peace like a river attends your soul, where once you felt like that burden would crash over you, suddenly you feel a sudden peace and quiet and from deep within you comes the thank you Jesus! Thank you Lord!

You have gotten your answer but it may not have revealed itself here on the earth yet.

Now let me tell you what to do next after experiencing this dimension of prayer....

CHAPTER FOUR
NOW YOU HAVE GOTTEN THE ANSWER TO YOUR PRAYER

*"Now this is the confidence that we
have in Him, that if we ask anything
according to His will, He hears us.
And if we know that He hears us,
whatever we ask, we know that we have
the petitions that we have asked of Him."*

-1st John 5:14-15

The experience you had above when you prayed the burden through and you started to laugh, sing, rejoice or all of a sudden felt the peace of the Lord after a moment of intense intercession was God speaking to you, telling you that He has heard your prayer.

That was Him telling you that your answer had been given and dispatched unto you... but you have to be careful at this stage because many people still do not receive in tangible form the answer they have received in the spiritual sense.

Here is how it works:

"Therefore I say to you, whatever

things you ask when you pray, believe
that you receive them, and you will have
them."

-Mark 11:24

This is the last principle of receiving answers when you pray; believe that you have received them and you shall have them.

You don't have before you receive; you receive before you have.

You must understand that that peace God gave you after you prayed the burden through was Him answering you even though you have not seen the physical manifestation yet; it is yours. So you believe that and then you would see the physical manifestation. You don't believe that God has already answered you when you prayed the burden through, and then the answer would never be yours. It is as simple as that.

I am now very familiar with this principle of answered prayers.

I remember the year 2019 when I was praying about going on a mission trip to Ghana and again I didn't know how it would all come together; with open doors, provision, funding and support. While praying God gave me the Isaiah 45 scripture and told me He had gone before me to open the doors before me and make my paths straight. Then He told me not to pray about it anymore. So I believed God that the road has been made for me to go to Ghana and every time I would think about it, I would praise and give thanks to God (that's the evidence that you believe, you switch to praise and thanksgiving). All the while I was doing this, I wasn't online, and a sister was helping me speak to contacts about the trip. By the time I came back from my retreat, the road had been cleared and all I did was show up to minister in Ghana. Praise the Lord!

But notice that all these came about because I had obeyed God to stop praying about it. If your answer has been given, then why are you still praying about the matter? Then that prayer becomes a sign of unbelief. The sign that you believe you have received when you prayed that burden through is that you switch to praise and thanksgiving.

Jesus also modelled this wisdom for us.

> *"Then they took away the stone from the place where the dead man was lying. And Jesus lifted up His eyes and said, "Father, I thank You that You have heard Me. And I know that You always hear Me, but because of the people who are standing by I said this, that they may believe that You sent Me." Now when He had said these things, He cried with a loud voice, "Lazarus, come forth!"*
>
> *-John 11:41-43*

I love this scripture for personal reasons because God has used it to speak to me a lot concerning receiving in the flesh what I have already gotten the answer for in prayer. A mighty miracle of raising a dead man back to life again was about to happen here and how it came to be was through thanksgiving. *Father, I thank you that you have heard me…* even before the physical manifestation of the miracle of raising Lazarus from the dead, Jesus already knew that this thing is DONE DEAL. I have prayed it through and at the sound of *thanksgiving;* the dead man came back to life.

So shall it be for you. The distance between answers received spiritually and answers tangibly manifested physically is your thanksgiving.

Thanksgiving shows that you have received and if you have received, then you shall have.

CONCLUSION

"Imitate me, just as I also imitate Christ."

-1st Corinthians 11:1

I have had someone ask me before to share how I pray with her; what do I do when I have a lot of things to pray about, to ensure that I pray about all of them with the time I have… I tried to answer her but I feel this book is a more comprehensive answer to that question. This is my prayer life that gets results in just a few chapters.

If you follow this life in prayer you would also get results. You will get answers that astound men. Family liberation and deliverance from the hand of the enemy would be gotten. There is nothing that cannot be received from heaven through the altar of prayer. The altar of prayer is the only legal way for receiving blessings from the hand of God and getting heaven to rule on your behalf.

You must familiarize yourself with the secret place of prayer, yield yourself in prayer to the burdens God places on your heart, pray them through in intercession and give thanks till what you have received shows up in tangible form upon the earth.

After you get one result through this process, then you go back over and over and over again. It is the only way we get the hand of the Judge of the whole earth to rule on our behalf.

It is my prayer that heaven responds as you reach out to Him (as He surely will) and may you have testimonies upon testimonies that strengthen your walk with God and makes you know 'I have history with God".

May God place burdens of prayer and intercession upon you and may you yield to become God's altar of prayer upon the earth in Jesus name, amen.

Lots of Love,

Hephzibah Frances,

Your Fellow Student of The School Of Prayer And Supplication.

Lagos, Nigeria,

20th January 2021.

PRAYER TO BE BORN AGAIN AND FILLED WITH THE SPIRIT

"But as many as received Him, to them He gave the right to become children of God, to those who believe in His name:"

-John 1:12

I need not tell you that the answer to prayer only goes to those who are sons and daughters of the King. The King gives power of rule and authority to His children. The main prayer God really wants to hear from a sinner (one who hasn't given his life to Jesus Christ) is the prayer for mercy and salvation.

Would God help an unbeliever if he prays to God for help or healing etc.? Yes He would. He would heal you even when you don't know Him as your God. That's His mercy at work but as far as wielding authority in prayer that changes things on the earth like we have talked about, you can't. Only sons of God are given that authority through Christ Jesus. Jesus Christ the head of the church is the only one who has the authority over heaven and the earth given to Him by the Father God. Jesus gives it to us because we are sons of God and the body of Christ, attached to Him as the head. So therefore if you aren't attached to Him, you cannot wield authority over demons and situations in prayer.

The seven sons of Sceva tried to use authority over demons without belonging to God and the demons beat them black and blue.

Acts 19:11-20

English Standard Version

The Sons of Sceva

11 And God was doing extraordinary miracles by the hands of Paul, 12 so that even handkerchiefs or aprons that had touched his skin were carried away to the sick, and their diseases left them and the evil spirits came out of them. 13 Then some of the itinerant Jewish exorcists undertook to invoke the name of the Lord Jesus over those who had evil spirits, saying, "I adjure you by the Jesus whom Paul proclaims." 14 Seven sons of a Jewish high priest named Sceva were doing this. 15 But the evil spirit answered them, "Jesus I know, and Paul I recognize, but who are you?" 16 And the man in whom was the evil spirit leaped on them, mastered all of them and overpowered them, so that they fled out of that house naked and wounded. 17 And this became known to all the residents of Ephesus, both Jews and Greeks. And fear fell upon them all, and the name of the Lord Jesus was extolled.

Does God know you? Only if you belong to Him can He share the authority that makes darkness and demons flee away from you. We can then use His authority in prayer.

Would you like to give your life to Christ Jesus?

It's simple.

"But what does it say? "The word is near you, in your mouth and in your heart"

> *(that is, the word of faith which we*
> *preach): that if you confess with your mouth the*
> *Lord Jesus and believe in your heart*
> *that God has raised Him from the dead,*
> *you will be saved*
>
> *-Romans 10:8-9*

Believe in your heart that Jesus is Lord and confess with your mouth and you shall be saved.

Pray these words below:

> *Lord Jesus I come to you today. I ask you to have mercy upon me, save me from my sins. Forgive me for my iniquities. I believe that you are the son of God and I receive you as Lord and savior over my life. Come into my heart and fill me with your Holy Spirit. Thank you Lord for saving me, in Jesus name I have prayed, amen.*

Congratulations! But I want you to know that that is not the end.

First of all, get this discipleship eBook we put out for free for you to help you grow in Christ.

Get it free on:

Amazon

Okadabooks

Smashwords

Bambooks

Then listen to me: *there is more!*

After Jesus died and rose from the dead, He told the disciples about receiving the most important part of their walk with Him… THE HOLY GHOST!

He said:

> *"And being assembled together with*
> *them, He commanded them not to*
> *depart from Jerusalem, but to wait for*
> *the Promise of the Father, "which," He*
> *said, "you have heard from Me;*

for John truly baptized with water, but
you shall be baptized with the Holy Spirit
not many days from now."
Therefore, when they had come
together, they asked Him, saying, "Lord,
will You at this time restore the kingdom
to Israel?"
And He said to them, "It is not for you
to know times or seasons which the
Father has put in His own authority.
But you shall receive power when the
Holy Spirit has come upon you; and you
shall be witnesses to Me in Jerusalem,
and in all Judea and Samaria, and to the
end of the earth."

-Acts 1:4-8

You cannot survive as a believer without being filled with the Holy Ghost who is the power of God. You can be a believer but still terribly weak in spirit and cannot stand to dispense authority in the earth without the power of the Holy Ghost.

Jesus fulfilled this promise of sending His Spirit to us in Acts chapter 2:

"When the Day of Pentecost had fully come, they were all with one accord in one place. And suddenly there came a sound from heaven, as of a rushing mighty wind, and it filled the whole house where they were sitting. Then there appeared to them divided tongues, as of fire, and one sat upon each of them. And they were all filled with the Holy Spirit and began to speak with other tongues, as the Spirit gave them utterance."

-Acts 2:1-4

You should read the whole book of Acts and see how these men after being filled with the Holy Spirit were raising the dead back to life, healing the sick and performing miracles by the power of the Spirit. This is also the kind of believer God wants you to be; filled with His power to do wonders upon the earth and to walk as Jesus upon the earth.

Now, just as you received salvation which is a gift and not of works, so also you receive the Holy Ghost as a gift from the Lord as He has already been given unto us.

*Lift up your hands right now, and say these words: **"Father I thank you for the gift of the Holy Spirit. I thank you for sending Him to live in us. Lord I thank you for this gift. I now receive your gift of the Holy Spirit. Holy Spirit, come upon me, fill me up to overflowing. I wholly receive you in Jesus name amen.'***

Now continue to thank the Lord for the gift of the Holy Spirit; open your mouth, thank Him and you may hear some sounds bubbling up in your belly. Open your mouth and just begin to speak them out without feeling self-conscious. It is the language of the Spirit. Keep speaking and try to schedule at least one hour of praying in tongues a day. That's where the power is.

I would love to hear your experience with God if you gave your life to Him or got filled with the Spirit from this book, email okorofrances@gmail.com

Keep growing in Christ!

I love you!

EXCERPT FROM THE CHRISTIAN FICTION BOOK –
"NEW BEGINNINGS"

Massachusetts, U.S.A

January 2019

Sophia looked at her god-forsaken trailer-park house. The place was old, just like she felt herself..

Old. Old hen, old cat. *Same ol' same ol'.*

She looked up at the ceiling to an imaginary place she didn't dare mention. And though she was just coming from church, she didn't dare speak to Him; she was mad at Him and wasn't on talking terms with Him who she once called the lover of her soul.

The angels sat clustered around Sophia as they whispered among themselves, "she doesn't even know that she is in a test does she?"

"No she doesn't". Clem whispered back. He was the oldest of the angels in terms of rank and they all had gathered here tonight as the last showdown between the kingdom of darkness and the Kingdom of Light and Sophia, precious Sophia was their middle ground. When she awoke again tomorrow, the battle line would have been drawn. She either would have the new or have the old; she couldn't have both.

And for the sake of Papa God, Clem hoped that she would choose right.

***

As Sophia slept that night she literally felt as though a brick had been thrown at her head. Clem sat by her bedside, powerless to do anything except she bid him come.

He and his other angel mates were here for her but she wouldn't have them work except she invited Father in and she had declared that she and Father were not on speaking terms for now. That was okay, the Father always laughed at Such things. Clem looked at her tenderly; this lovely one who the Father Himself loved.

Sophia could feel words and songs arising from the inside of her but for the life of her she couldn't bring herself to sing them. She was too hurt; her wound was still too raw and painful for her to sing. Unbidden, her tears began to flow as she thought about all that had happened within the space of a year.

She had received a prophetic word for new seasons and believed it with her whole heart. On

the basis of that word and what she felt the
Lord told her, she had moved to the new town of
Massachusetts. Massachusetts stood for
freedom but she had had the most bound year
of her life if she may say so herself. One thing fast on
the
heels of the other had happened.
First her fiancé of three years had left her, then
she lost the new job she had seemingly already
gotten but slipped right out of her fingers. The
job was the reason why she had the biggest
green light to move to the new city but as it was,
that too was gone and they didn't even give her
the courtesy of telling her that the job was gone
so she was left hanging for weeks. The Lord
opened a door and she started getting requests
to babysit for the women at Church and that's
been how her bills had managed to be paid for
the whole year. Yes, she would concede that He
opened the door but it was nothing close to
what she was expecting.

Who says a word like new beginnings and then

brings a babysitting job as the fulfillment of

that word? The distance was too far off away

 from

each other. Too far off.

Everything had fallen right back side up as soon as that
word was given to

her and to make it worse nothing had yet

happened to her – nothing that she would

consider new.

All of a sudden she heard a voice saying , *"come*

let me show you the science of new beginnings".

This was the time Clem had been waiting for,

he and his colleagues had been sent to Sophia

last night to open up things she didn't know to her.

The Father had seen her last night praying,

"Lord, I do not know what to do, I do not know what to

think but please tell me and show me what to do".

Her prayer had kick-started a response from

the heavenlies and they were here in response

 to that prayer. The Lord had sent them to open   unto

her the science of *New Beginnings.*

***

- **NEW BEGINNINGS BY HEPHZIBAH FRANCES IS AVAILABLE ON Online sites.**
- **Find it on:**

Amazon

Okadabooks

Smashwords

Bambooks

ABOUT THE AUTHOR

Hephzibah Frances is a child of God and the Lord's delight. She is a certified Lawyer, an author and a Christian Blogger. As a Social Entrepreneur, she is the founder of *Awakening Youthful Seeds for Christ initiative (AYSCAFRICA)*

She is also the founder of *The Women at The Well Ministries,* a Christian ladies ministry passionate about raising women filled with Jesus (@TWTWINTER-NATIONAL on social media) She is the CEO of *Beautiful Feet Publishing* (beautifulfeetpublishing@gmail.com, a publishing house that exists to help aspiring authors' birth their books to life, holding workshops and available email courses to help authors self-publish their own books, as well as providing ISBN services for authors.

She believes that she is a scribe for the Lord, called to write words of healing and wisdom to her generation and her writing gift is meant to be used for Jesus. She enjoys travelling and sight-seeing adventures, and she hopes to travel the world in an all-expense paid trip someday.

CONNECT WITH HEPHZIBAH FRANCES VIA THE FOLLOWING CHANNELS:

Twitter: **@HephzibahFran**

Instagram: **@HephzibahFrances**

Facebook: www.facebook.com/AuthorHephzibahfrances

Blog: www.hephzibahfrances.com

READ OTHER BOOKS BY THE HEPHZIBAH

HEPHZIBAH FRANCES
chastity
RIPE MARITAL
PR♡MISES
BY HEPHZIBAH FRANCES

FICTION BOOKS

- **ALL BOOKS BY HEPHZIBAH FRANCES ARE AVAILABLE ON Online sites.**
- **Find her books on:**

Amazon

Okadabooks

Smashwords

Bambooks

Leave Reviews, tag and follow Hephzibah Frances on Instagram

- here --- > http://www.instagram.com/HephzibahFrances
- You can also call. Text or/and WhatsApp +2347035539092 to reach the author to order for bulk purchases of her book, or/and reach her for other discussions.
- Email for her books: *Hephzibahfrancesbooks@gmail.com*
- *Email for personal discussions: okorofrances@gmail.com*

JOIN BOOKS BY HF LAUNCH TEAM

READ BOOKS BY HEPHZIBAH FRANCES FOR FREE AND HELP SHARE THEM TO THE NATIONS.

JOIN THE GROUP FOR FREE HERE.

9 798700 610476